Uprock Headspin Scramble and Dive

POEMS

PATRICK ROSAL

A Karen & Michael Braziller Book
PERSEA BOOKS / NEW YORK

Persea Books, Inc.
853 Broadway
New York, NY 10003

Library of Congress Cataloging-in-Publication Data

Rosal, Patrick, 1969-
Uprock headspin scramble and dive : poems / Patrick Rosal.
      p. cm.
"A Karen & Michael Braziller Book."
ISBN 0-89255-293-X (pbk. : alk. paper)
1. Filipino Americans—Poetry. I. Title.
PS3618.O774 U67 2003
811'.6—dc21

                          2002156299

Design by Rita Lascaro
Typeset in Cheltenham

Printed in the United Stated of America.

for Inang . . .

and all the names I never knew you by

Contents

ONE

TWO

Acknowledgements

I'd like to extend gratitude to the following publications in which some poems in this collection previously appeared: *Lumina, Folio, Sarah Lawrence Review, Columbia: A Journal of Literature and Art, The Literary Review, North American Review, Babaylan Speaks* (online); and the anthologies *Beacon Best 2001, Screaming Monkeys,* and *Eros Pinoy.*

I would particularly like to acknowledge Phebe Davidson at Palanquin Press who published my chapbook *Uncommon Denominators*, in which several of these poems originally appeared.

I am also grateful to The Atlantic Center for the Arts, Penn State Altoona's Emerging Writer in Residency, and Bloomfield College for providing time and resources, which made the completion of this book possible.

And many, many thanks to the following individuals who, in varying roles, have given me unwavering and indispensable support: Paul Genega, Gabriel Fried, John Carey, Sandy Van Dyk, Thomas Lux, Joan Larkin, Suzanne Gardinier, Vijay Seshardi, Marie Howe, Ross Gay, Curtis Bauer, Jon Wei, Lee Peterson, Elaine Sexton, Alex Socarides, Paul Schaeffer, Jeet Thayil, Alex Traugott, Leslieann Hobayan, Junot Díaz, Carleton Dunn, Asheba Brown, Nicole Dupree, Luis Francia, Eric Gamalinda, Nick Carbó, Denise Duhamel, Eileen Tabios, Bino Realuyo, Quincy Troupe. And the fam: Anthony, Mark, Christine, Katrina (idi ken itan), Phil, Junji, Jo-Jo, Erwin, Joyce, Anne, Monica, Janis, Joy, Chris, Steve, Tee, G-Mon, Deez, Hex, Boodz, Big Ben, Joel, Jeremy, Brigante, Kim, Teej, Joanna, MD, Patty, Carlisa, Atee, Tia, May, Honey, Kat B, Chrissi, Ray, Wally, Steph, A-Roc, Jay, Stunt, Marianne, Cool Jeff Factor, Lia, Shaun, Cleon, Mike, Kisha, Adrian, Chuck, Dazz, Alex, Alan, DeeJay Jayvee, DeeJay AJ. One Love Love Many.

Dream-singers,

Story-tellers,

Dancers,

Loud laughers in the hands of Fate—

—Langston Hughes

one

B-BOY INFINITIVES

To suck until our lips turned blue
the last drops of cool juice
from a crumpled cup sopped
with spit the first Italian Ice of summer
To chase popsicle stick skiffs
along the curb skimming stormwater
from Woodbridge Ave. to Old Post Road
To be To B-boy To be boys who
snuck into a garden to pluck
a baseball from mud and shit
To hop that old man's fence before
he bust through his front door
with a lame-bull limp charge
and a fist the size of half a spade
To be To B-boy To lace shell-toe Adidas
To say Word to Kurtis Blow
To laugh the afternoons
someone's mama was so black
when she stepped out the car
the oil light went on
To count hairs sprouting
around our cocks To touch
ourselves To pick the half-smoked
True Blues from my father's ashtray
and cough the gray grit
into my hands To run
my tongue along the lips of a girl
with crooked teeth To be
To B-boy To be boys for the ten days
an 8-foot gash of cardboard lasts
after we dragged it

seven blocks then slapped it
on the cracked blacktop To spin
on our hands and backs To bruise
elbows wrists and hips To Bronx-Twist
Jersey version beside the mid-day traffic
To swipe To pop To lock freeze and
drop dimes on the hot pavement—
even if the girls stopped watching
and the street lamps lit buzzed all
night we danced like that
and no one called us home

FREDDIE

Freddie claimed lineage from the tough
Boogie-Down Boricuas
who taught him how to break-
dance on beat: up-
rock headspin scramble and dive

We called it a suicide:
the front-flip B-boy move that landed you
back flat on the blacktop That
was Freddie's specialty—the way he'd jump
into a fetal curl mid-air then *thwap*
against the sidewalk—his body
laid out like the crucified
Jesus he knocked down
one afternoon in his mom's bedroom
looking for her extra purse
so both of us could shoot
asteroids and space invaders
until dusk
        That wasn't long before
Freddie disappeared
then returned one day as someone else's ghost
smoked-out on crack
singing *Puerto Rico Puerto Rico*
las chicas de Puerto Rico
That was the first summer we believed
you had to be good at something
so we stood around and watched
Freddie on the pavement—all day—
doing suicides
until he got it right

NINE THOUSAND OUTLINES

If every story has its beginning
this one starts in the armpit of a god—the plots
of fishbone and vinegar a history of nails
a war or two a swan some saints of course some
slaves Eventually boys one day
toss bricks at a burst of starlings
then plash through the sky gathered
in potholes and oil-slick rainpuddles And
there is—that afternoon—a girl
awkward and pale crossing the lot
among scattered genuflections of sedans
and wagons The cooked rubber
fumes the projects when
those boys' necks erect and everything
sunstruck for a moment
become still

When I say I was once a boy who became
a wolf who became a crow who turned
to salt I mean I've become a man somehow
without remembering that girl: stork-
awkward and pale When I say
the boys are my friends I mean
all it takes is one of us startled
into quickness: a twitch
of the hip the others follow
and the girl—a contraption of wings—
stumbles for the nearest door

Some of you want to know
Some of you have already imagined

the short corridors the scramble up
each flight the landing where the girl cornered
raises her head once
to spit at the crotches crowded around
Do the boys drown themselves
or do they merely wet their snouts until
she becomes the river they want
Do you and I agree
these boys—when they're done—turn
grab their cocks (still hard)
then laughing emerge
into a parking lot now doused
in the dusk's chemical bloom

She'll still be there: slumped in a hallway
where I leave her so you can
cross the lot climb the stairs and see for yourself
It no longer smells like piss
It's a place where a girl can cower her whole life
where things have flung themselves
so far into the future time already reels backward
where twilight etches—in patinas
older than bone—9,000 outlines
of a girl whose endings I've traveled this far to forget
with all the lies a boy will work a lifetime to believe
until he's caught looking back

LAZARUS

Jesus the air is so thick
                    and I'm drowning
in my own sight in the bright black
streets in the dawn
                    breaking like riptides
and how I need
                    even against
the nights' stunned canopy
your name
            to cry out   need
a curse a reason to open my mouth Jesus
        without scripture without healing
without the bone-
                    slow sway of a city's steel
        and satellites
beaming wineskins without wine and Jesus
                    the air is so thick I want you
to hold Jesus out
                    your muddy Jesus thumbs
and touch my eyes
                    to make me Jesus blind

A GOOD DAY

On a good day two hands aren't enough
to feel the world says Hector—my friend
who more than once has beat another man
until both arms—fatigued—limp
two numb slabs of meat
flung from his torso

Last week some man runs Hector off the road
wrongly accusing him of feeling
the world—in particular
the secret regions of this man's wife—
a claim which Hector calmly denies
But when the guy calls my friend a spic
Hector bashes him dumb
as a window pane leaving the dazed stranger
nose-down in the slow lane of a Jersey interstate
Every time it comes to fists Hector believes
he exacts revenge for an afternoon ten years ago
five other boys battered him into a week-long sleep

How many of you live like this: hoping
to run—as a kind of faith—
one by one into the five people
you hold accountable for your lifelong spite
some guy you'd rather not imagine too clearly
target dummy for your unspent passions
practice for the apocalyptic day
you're supposed to settle
some school-kid epic sparked
amid the cranial echoes of a gym
so you barter your only pair of arms

for the slabs of meat dangled from your shoulders
a trade which leaves you for now
two hands short of the body
you failed to feel the world with
in the first place
                    Today Hector's in bed
propped like a mannequin
a cyst jammed near his spine
Every movement ends in a stiff wince
To make his thirty-foot trek to the toilet
I have to help all 220 pounds of agony
onto its feet In a couple weeks
Hector will be well enough
to lift his mother
out of the noose
she will fashion and hang
from her bedroom ceiling
But first Hector's hands will clasp
around the back of my neck
my hands on his hips
until we're standing face to face
trying not to break
the fragile plane between us
like two sixteen year olds at the last dance
heads down
hands full
and holding on

YOU CLUBHOUSE BOYS

You Clubhouse Boys who
dance on the third knuckle
from the sun
      my heels burn
from the hell we help build
How many of us
      slit our hands
happy in the knife-glint scuffle
How many of us taste
the raw red rock
      in our chests
How many sing
      the *hilot's* song
spilled into New Brunswick streets
drunk with a borrowed liquor
we call time
      In this world
there is no act of contrition
and there is only
      this world
So I raise a glass to broken heads
and dead ones
      and new ones
born with fists
      to the murderers
and the murderers' grief
I raise a glass to blacktop drag
steeltoe thumb-toke
      I raise a glass
to side-sway
      I raise a glass

to the gun
        I raise a glass
to the metallic tang of blood
in the cheek
        I raise a glass
to the pipes and blacked-out windows
to back walls tagged up
              torn down
to pulse-code bass
nightflash and deepthump ether
we sleep under like
          crashing waves
I raise my glass to you:
who stumble this far
          smoke scarred
fire stoked stoneblast
I raise a glass and count
          how many
with dropped scabbed hands
are still left standing

for CHP

THE NEXT HUNDRED-ODD
HALF-DREAMED MILES

This part's real: the kid sways
near a curb (the club's fuck-hard
flash of neon lights keeps time
inside) his top lip split
mouth popped into hellglow blossom
eyes swelled shut like peaches
Small half-as-dark and twice
as yapping drunk as you
he swings forward and lands
a clean right cross you confuse
with a good reason to try
and toss him like a sack of trash
into the midnight traffic
His Pinay girlfriend (so light-skinned
and round-eyed she would have passed
for Magellan's daughter) shouts
You goddamned monkey in perfect English
which makes you hold
his head in your hands
—without thinking of his mother
cursing in Tagalog—
when you thrust one more time
the tender cartilage of his nose
against your knee except
this story isn't about you It's about me
and every time someone's bar-buzz
crescendos to mezzo-forte tough-guy
maybe I should consider that kid
holding both arms out as if he'd catch
whatever he could summon from the sky

but rage doesn't work like that
It's like this: I race down the Parkway
and skip every exit I know too well
slumped in the driver's seat
for the next hundred-odd half-dreamed miles
taking turns sucking my bloody knuckle
with the only girl I think I'll ever kiss
—my tongue too dumb to tell
which taste belongs to whom
and which mouth happens when

RITUAL FROM THE BOOK OF MISTAKES

Take away the man
who helps his father put a .22
dead center between a steer's eyes
and you take away the man who
turns his back before the knifeblade
breaks the tender hide of the beast's throat
Take away the man who swings forward
shoveling his way through
a wagon topped off with feed
and you take away the man
who sways as though he moves with all
his weight all the weight of fathers
and half the lineage of mothers behind him
Take away this man
and his boys—whom he will beat
before any one of them becomes the fool
he has promised to leave
brawling the streets overseas
and you take away the man
who once lay down in another country
with a woman whose name
he hasn't said aloud in twenty years

Unless you've stood beside this man
who shouldn't be standing
who nine times got up and walked
out of wrecks and falls
gunfire and love
who's held up by a spine
these days more back than bone
Unless you've seen him kiss

his full-grown son on the cheek
and embrace him long enough
to pray for grace from a god he's cursed
once a week for forty years
you might not think of what it means
to drive to the highest point in Helixville
where he stops to overlook the hard farm roads
fallow fields and barroom arias of his life
Unless you've swung a hammer beside him
his body braced—without a flinch—
against a joist to hold it straight
you might not understand
why it only takes a splinter in the thumb
to make him lie down
for a day and a half with fever
and why he might cry like a little girl
which is what he would not want
because goddammit he is not a man
until you sit in his pick-up truck and smell
the beer and cigarettes of seven generations
and you spend the hour-plus drive
in the kind of long silences only shared
between dear friends or dire enemies
or brothers This is the problem
You won't know how to thank him
The Lord giveth and the Lord taketh away

for Clyde Lasure

CITRUS CITY

When I walk down Second Avenue
                        the first
sun-spent day of spring
                        and the scent of dropped
flowers spilled bottles of OE and mints
begins to burn from the asphalt and people
strip to the waist reminded of some first urge
to be naked against the city air
                        (eight million breaths
at any given moment)
                        I see a boy devour
the last slice of an orange
                        and my mouth waters
so I buy one for myself
at the closest stand The citrus drips
down my wrists
                        from the corners of my lips
and I realize it's been some time
                        since this joy: since
I've peeled and eaten an orange on the street
and it's been some time
                        since I've seen anyone
eat an orange outside
I look into the eyes of Manhattanites who
look me in the mouth
                        and I think: perhaps she
tastes the same
tart under her tongue and maybe
she will head straight for a fruit stand and buy
a navel to eat on the street too
                        and someone

will see her or two people will see her love her skirt
sprayed with the minuscule burst of juice
so they buy lots of oranges

                               eat one on the bus heading
uptown (toward all those oranges
in the Bronx) and the person stepping off
at twenty-third walks crosstown to Chelsea
surrenders his organic nut bar

                              stops at a fruit stand
and maybe someone en route to Chinatown
bumps into the guy from Chelsea
and remembers his

                    first orange

                          at a picnic
as a child

          on a beach—

                  in the Philippines—

                          in August
So he buys two oranges

                  goes home to his lover
whose drape of sweat

              smells like the day
and since he's already eaten one along the way
they sit across from each other

                and share
the remaining one:

              its packed flesh a brief but cool
reprieve from their apartment

                  steaming like an engine
and this is how a whole city's

              eating oranges:
the first sun-spent spring day—

                an orgy of them

LINWOOD

To show me the years he's hauled his body's freight
through the city streets he removes his shoes and socks—
one toe on each arthritic foot green and limp as the tip
of a boiled asparagus—his soles' soursweet funk
I sit close enough to Linwood to spit into his beard
or kiss him on the cheek Between brown-bag swigs
he says his brother returns every night alive:
from Guantánamo Johannesburg sometimes Saigon
He professes to dream—through the ancient eyes
of Timbuktu Rome Detroit—everything
I know (which is almost nothing) about Curtis Mayfield
an African moon and the time it takes to sink
to the bottom of a river where the light is brighter only
when you close your eyes

I misquote Neruda He hums Jobim over a four/four
groove he slaps across his knee clapping a doubletime
        backbeat
until the two of us slur and stomp and thrum
and maybe for a moment there is a song
between us a black man without a home and a tone-deaf
        chink
each drunk each enchanted out of time in his own bruised
        music
Before I stagger to my feet he takes my hand in his
        so thick
and coarse it feels like my palm should burn against it
        and he says
Goodbye Beloved

One winter I might curse him amid faces
cast like dark marble mumbling for a quarter
For all I know among the trash and dung he sleeps well
some nights With the grace of whatever gods
may he refuse affections thrown into the street
like morsels of sweet corn May he one day curse
a good pair of ugly socks and a cold pint of imported beer
May he read his name in a letter from a woman who
into his lips *Desafinado* sings May he recite the hard
        bargains of love—
Linwood—part carcass part king

WHO SAYS THE EYE LOVES SYMMETRY

Doesn't the eye love the ragged
tear of sky the treetop-shred
horizon The eye—after all—
loves the dizzy
dip of a road: its precarious
tilt towards a ravine
only wrist-deep water
and giant smooth rocks to break
the sky's fall The eye
loves the bit peach window agape
buildings caught mid-swagger across a skyline
The eye loves unpainted pickets
cracked planks the harlequin the prow
poked out of water
like a chin loves
the evergreen arched over a flood
like an old man looking into the street
for a hand loves a sawed link chewed
rope a birch's slants But
the eye can't
love what it can't
see: the woman
striding tired and brave amid the lobby's bustle
and under her shirt
a single breast

For Maureen Clyne

A PRAYER AT THE EDGE OF THE MAP

When I see a child—struck by a car—stand
then stagger until he drops on the sidewalk
his sister screaming nothing I can hear
over the Delco blare of a local station
the high din of slapped bells circles in my skull:
a radio hum the sirens—how soon it's all gone

For once this drive's revised its highways to the usual
squat blocks of kids whacking a Spaldeen
the tom-tom cadence of basketballs
gray-matter rags heaped beside a Honda
dropped tinted and waxed pumping hip hop
But soon I'll pass this too

Whatever hauls my life across this moment
then this one—ancestral stir/earned agony—
grant that there are tongue wind
to rile the streets and a god
to scrawl his human name on our backs

ODE TO EDISON, NJ

Look at these dozen boys—
stoned purple/juked
out of shoes the slow
shameless quake of their body's reggae
thirteen colors or more poised
against the chain-links of your uncut outfields
gravel lots and b-ball courts
See the cee-lo player's
fist: the fractured
rattle of dice like
polished bone Tonight
they'll stagger outside town
from bar to burger joint
run by the sons of men who once spoke
the secret slur of Mediterranean thieves

Where are your ecstatic babblers
in their smocks Where
are the women eloquent
without feet Where are your pedestrians
crawling amok There's a darkness
jammed down your throat
Where are your ghosts
your fiends your voracious
lovers How awkward
how small a town
for Elks Where is the terrible
crack of a man straining
out of his range to sing
I ain't got no woman
I ain't got no Amen

Edison you are not Loisaida or Princeton/
Tampa or Tripoli/Paris or Santiago
You are the land of strip
malls and Tastee Subshop: here
are the makers of heroes You
are bastards and cruel
and you are blessed
and some day you will know this

THE SMOKEDRIFT

Another chunk of black lacquered wood
thrown into the fire conjures a noxious stink
Who wouldn't get drunk under a dusk like this
I squeeze shadows into my fists
until each hand holds a night of its own
Into the blaze I sling slab after splintered slab
what's left of a piano I once played
before my cousin James lugged it to the driveway
and smashed it with a sledge hammer It stayed
in his living room for nine months under dust
most of its notes a bad twang
or low oak thunk toneless
as a bat slugged against a neighbor's bed
My fingers couldn't touch
a blues cool enough to burn me to my elbows
Even if I had the courage to plunge wrist deep
into these embers I couldn't save the piano
too much for James' hourly wage
to fix or tune It's like a song a man surely dead
might have remembered suddenly
in one of those short talks across
the border between two backyards: one man
tapping his tobacco pipe on the lawn mower handle
the other painting his garage—one man
explaining to the other (ten years in a country
he will never grow to love): this land
used to be a farm and every other house on the block
built with his own two hands—a fact useless
to the child listening nearby who has yet to do anything
with his own two hands even learn
from a black kid named Derek a few gospel chords

to the last verse in the third song on the B-Side of some
Richard Smallwood album before
they hop the back fence to kung-fu chop
every maple sapling in a four-yard radius
One day one of these boys will
pull a woman close in a candlelit shed for
he knows not what he does
and one day both will see their friend
a ghost white as rocks cracked
from a vial the moment before a flame
unravels its magic smoke and licks
the inside of his skull—an image
years later the first child might want to set fire to
with a few last chunks of wood: what used to be a leg
or soundboard or scuffed lid returning
to the air in soot its unsung Hallelujahs
or else a Mighty Fortress is Our God but by then
he's no longer a child
and by now the kindling's all ash
Eleven friends have joined James and me
We fling—to keep the small blaze living—
bits of everything: pine needles cigarettes and twigs
letters books and lumber from the basement
unfinished We even toss into the flames
bottles coins and nails we know will never burn
We huddle around the heat None poor or hungry
at this moment There isn't one who doesn't laugh
even my cousin James the dark one with eyes
like lead who knows what it's like to stand
at the edge of a small emptiness
cast as his own body in sleep
the one place where everything must become
rain in order to be true

He's piss drunk and I
believe him when he says *Fools
only answer to a darkness
sweeter than their own
but every darkness is their own*
This could be any summer
We could by any fools
We sit around a fire and sing
and no one knows the words
We make them up
We drink whiskey
and smoke

AS I READ ETHERIDGE KNIGHT
FOR THE FIRST TIME

I pull in my elbows pull in
my knees I think I take up
more space than I deserve

in my own skin and the floorboard
moans quicken and my heart
wants to catch up I feel

my throat move my tongue snap
against the roof of my mouth
but I know it's his voice his

reasons his love done got up and
left and made him want to sing
like he was up high swinging

from a crow's wing and I know
I know 'cause I hear it I hear it
clear as a bone drum I hear

the air split like a sea before my lips
and it's his voice his reasons his
love I hear him gnaw on a wedge

of moonlight in his cell all that rubble
in his belly and him making room
making room and saying out loud:

shake the dust   dust
stomp your feet   feet
straighten up and   fuck it man fly

For Ross Gay

NEXT

We used to share the holiest
of sacraments: opening
each other's beer then forgetting by dawn
whose bottle was whose
We used to envy that
handsome bastard for his looks
at least for his girl—definitely for his game
in the low post and two-handed dunk

Out of the hospital ward
—out of prison altogether—
for the first time in years Ariben's not
in a wheelchair
sporting an ugly smock
no more Bible meetings
no more cell block gossip
We might have visited him for
one free hour in the last decade
I could have written one
stinking letter Instead
we stand in the rain
our feet sinking
into someone else's grave

Ari-ben's in his casket
and three dozen people crowd
under a tarp meant for five
The guys next to us joke
about buzzer beaters and the crossover
how the good ones fade away

The thing is—some day we will die
We just don't know this yet
Or maybe I do
but in a week I'll forget
because the girl I'm supposed to spend
the rest of my life with
is getting drunk with someone
better than me She must think
she'll live forever too

Today you think you've learned
the difference between luck
and dying: You buy yourself
your sixth stiff drink
and toast our dead friend
You babble to a stranger at the bar
who makes you feel
beautiful You step outside
Like most days this one
only leads to the next Someone
might take this all for granted
No one said it should be you

For Phil, Erwin, and Chris

two

NOTES FOR THE UNWRITTEN BIOGRAPHY
OF MY FATHER, AN EX-PRIEST

You have to be born in San Vicente
a town lit by kerosene lamps searchlights and gunfire
where the ilustrados still speak Spanish
where the maids might look like your sisters
if they bathed every day
if they dropped to their knees
to pray rather than scrub
with coconut husks your floors
You have to be old enough to want to kiss a girl
but never say so The Japanese have to order
farmers to calisthenics at dawn
and you have to eat the best parts of a dog
and not know it

You have to enter the seminary
your mother proud her son will love God more
than he loves her and one brother
will die by bludgeon another
by bayonet having dug
his own grave before you can read
The Lord is my shepherd
I shall not want and you have to want
to be a lawyer like your father
but blessed and ordained you fast every night recite
Aquinas in Latin then fly
Stateside where you must pretend
you don't love miniskirts and blondes
big meals and comfortable beds
before Kennedy's dead
Martin's in Birmingham

Malcolm's in Mecca
and all those long-hairs just
want to make love not war

Maybe in Chicago you have to slip
a dress off the shoulders of a woman
from the province north of yours
which means she will know the distance between
Ay-ayaten ka and *I love you* sometimes
equals half the circumference
of the earth The woman's name
is Mimi who phones the rectory
after midnight to tell you she'll have your son
and before you marry her you'll creep
out her front door into the middle of the night
toward Gary then Brooklyn
and you still say mass/give penance/love
other women and you pray
theologians are right
about purgatory and prayer

But here your memory must cloud itself
so whom you love you love
in secret even your children
and Mimi—your wife—
whose grave you visit
to say things you'd never tell her in life

This is your story

This is your son These

are our sins
         and how
did we ever get here
            without them

ASBURY PARK, 1977

Why my mother didn't take me to school
that morning I couldn't figure out Clip-on
plaid double Windsor knot at my throat

a fat sandwich in my lunch box—
my mother and I that morning drove off
as my father cursed from the driveway

At boardwalk's end the Ferris wheel turned
like a cog catching its teeth in the overcast
Even the water was giant gadgetry

cranking onto the sand then
unsheathing itself from the shore and the sky
—like a gray stage curtain snagged half way—hung

If someone finally freed it I thought
it would reveal the ocean's secret
machinery suspended overhead

My mother said little just paid the man
for the taffy and hot dogs Our footsteps
on the broad wood planks sounded something

like work the uneven rhythm of building
—though I wasn't sure By noon I propped
my cheek against the rust-chipped railing

I watched the distant apparatus of breakers
rolling in and out under the gull-gashed wind
I looked up at my mother still silent and clasped

her hand: cool as the metal against my face
The moment she turned and I followed
I knew we'd be going back

THREE HOURS

I suppose despair is having
nothing to do: no two-week laundry no rent
to ignore no commute or evening news
no romance slanted against
a blush dusk swelling
behind the smokestacks and Pulaski Skyway
It's having to wait like a man
who stares at a screen—for three hours—
above the bed where his mother lies:
four lines bounce and dip then flat
and a nurse says *That's it*

For three hours despair is like that:
waiting in an ICU
with nothing to do—nothing
strapped so tight under your ribcage
you'd crack your own sternum to breathe
but you don't because what's made you
wait for three hours
sets you back on the track headed
full tilt toward nothing of your own so you hope
some day your son or daughter
despises nothing enough to stare
at a screen above your bed despairing
nothing to do and—for three hours—waits

For my brothers Anthony and Mark

A RIFF FOR MY MOTHER

I got drunk dizzy for days
                    after my mother's death For weeks
she lay on a dim-lit bed where I held her hand

a rotting fruit
                    its dank sweetness rising like a prayer toward
St. John's god's palms iron-cold pried open

for paradise
                    You see? I ain't right—forgetting
on whiskey and jazz how
                    I've wanted to be a man anywhere
but here
          how I've wanted a life measured
in extra innings
                    to be near a woman
who'll whisper to me *Baby* in a smoky room

Truth is
          I wanted time
And my mother never taught me
                    to stay awake
for church-loft Hosannas and acts of contrition
She taught me to speak of love
in 7silences I make up as I go along

30 JUNE 2000

The sun's cardiac through
the fog's gray gauze over the late bay
and tomorrow
you bury your father
your burly father
whose kind heart stopped still as a fist-
sized loaf of wine-sopped rye

Your grief is an old one
which means you're a man
which means there is time for you
—suddenly urged toward the sweet
switch of round summer dresses
and the thug pulse of late-night bomb-bomb bass—
to lean on the stone steps of a church
whose god you barely believe exists
There is time for the small
amazements of an ocean after a storm
time still for you and I
to strut along the usual streets
as if nothing could surprise us

and—Jose—there is time
to forgive the earth for failing to bear
its share of starved gracile children There is time
to mourn the weight
of a father's dwindling heart

In memory of Bob Aguirre

THE OVERNIGHT FERRY

Suppose your father is well enough
to bitch about his supper
and doesn't Suppose tonight
he dreams he's young again
—long before disease begins
its sideways walk through
the marrow in his spine—
Suppose in sleep he counts
among the red canoes
and topless sunbathers
a man licking the cool wine
off a woman's mouth despite a tourist
who out loud repeats *Libyan Sea*
reminding your father of
an American word for freedom Suppose
the overnight ferry hasn't begun
and wind on the Acropolis
comes in gusts like flying dolphins
Suppose your father is alive somewhere
next to you without the olive trees
of his childhood his fishing pole or
his mother's towels out to dry
Suppose you've heard some of this before
in your father's dream
and you *are* your father
alive somewhere
beside yourself

For Katherine and Nicolette

"MY MOTHER IS IN LOS ANGELES"

Mom I wonder if dying to you
might be like landing
in Los Angeles on a clear day in March
still dressed for the Jersey winter
a little confused by a sky uncut
by factories and the Pulaski Skyway
a little stunned by pedestrians
who wait patiently at crosswalks
Are you intrigued by lemons from trees
—how for four days this city hasn't rained

I wonder if like me you ask yourself
why nearly everyone is so goddamned gorgeous
if you have to learn your way
around the wide boulevards
if you ever get used to people
who stare a little too long
when you ask for directions
or order a glass of water
And do strangers recognize your accent
then ask for news from the living
and do you have time
to visit the ones they bury

Mom maybe some things
vaguely remind us of home:
the rasp of a bad starter in the driveway
sit-com re-runs or a clip of Thurman Munson
blocking a fifty-nine foot change-up in the dirt
or maybe there's a house much like ours
where you held a Bible and rosary

praying to some dark ancestral sternum
where you learned about the rage of aging
in the arms of a god who answers
to ten thousand names
and none of them the one on your lips

This morning I stood on a pier in Venice
walked in a circle
a cigarette pinched
between my forefinger and thumb
When I looked out at the Pacific
for a moment I believed
I was stretched across the saltwater
For a moment I believed I was dead
suddenly thinking I was someone else
thinking I could fall madly in love
with this one and this one

I met a girl today who says she regrets
not seeing her sister the day she died
and I have nothing to tell her except
My mother is in Los Angeles
and she manages to get around

For Liza Alegado

UNCOMMON DENOMINATORS

I add up the times I've fantasized about
women I've seen but never spoken to
and divide that by the hours
I drive past cemeteries and add again
the weight of breath in your mouth
measured in the ancient Tagalog word for *yes*
—but the number always comes out the same

So I subtract the moon
and the smell of incense on Good Friday
trying to connect Planck's Constant
to the quantum moment between
a candlelit flick and the back of your neck
setting aside my 7 dreams of having sex once
with Tyra Banks who tells me *God*
You Filipino guys know
how to make love to a woman
and even if I tally the 10,069
channels launched by satellites
which have an asymptotic relationship
to the count of stones cast
from a sinner's fist raised
to the power of eight million punch-clock
stiffs heading home late
still the number comes out the same
and when a beggar pirouettes
along an expressway's center lane
swearing this won't be his last
cigarette (smoke rising from
the rust in his moustache) I suddenly know
the acceleration of a falling body

has little to do with slipping
a mother into the ground or
a whole greater than the sum of its parts

And if you ask what I'm doing
with 7 loaves and 4 fish multiplied
by the root of a dried tamarind tree
or the coefficient of friction
of a bullet on the brink of a rib
or the number of clips emptied
into an unarmed Guinean man
on a dark Bronx stoop I'll tell you
I'm looking for the exact
coordinates of falling in love plus or minus
the width of a single finger
lost along the axis of your lips

AIZA

Where Your name
means *where*
in Madagascar—
the question
a man breathes along
the hips of his wife
in the bony
dark of Tuliara
Where Your name
means *where*
in Madagascar and so
should be written
in Malagasy Visaya Creole
—but not here . . . Here

your hair spills
on my lap like a thief's
riches and your hands
a pair of clumsy blessings
somewhere at the end
of your body Here
are broken bottles
and odd copper coins
as if I should compare them
to your eyes Here
you become a mouth
full of mango
and salt which makes me crave
the surf and speak
the word
which is a question

on an island
where children
dream of never finding
the same path back Your name
is on their lips You might say
we are ancestors
to a race of beings
who will understand the sea
is your own tongue
or heart or anything
we suspect is partly human
and they will know
to sail into it
you have to risk
drowning
though none of us
knows when

or where Your name means
where in Madagascar
to the man breathing
along the hips
of his wife your
name a litany
for those
in the dark
who love
to lose their way

THE ANCIENT BAGUIO DEAD

Far from Manila's marquees scrimmed
in exhaust
                    past squatter's piss-stained
huts and Spanish Garrison walls
past the provincial
                    church bells circling
above the drunken belches and a dog
wandering off with a rib
                    through
the markets where a woman sells
the local soda bottles and boiled balut
a road winds
                    (wide enough for one headlong
bike and an oncoming bus)
to a mountain city
                    where they wait
stone-colored stiff
in glass cases under museum light
                    the Baguio dead: mummies
naked except for bands
tattooed from ankle to knee
                    on forearms
like sleeves marks of a warrior
or wanderer or mother—one whose
elbows pull tight to her sides
knees tucked to her breast as if shivering
in the early morning chill
                    eyes peer
as if she would gash
through the clay that once encased her
                    wheel through

the canopy of trees
                    tropic cool and dithered
with bird-flits and monkey tails
as if—crouched—about to smack
some sky god fattening himself on mist
This woman's lips
                    parted the width of a finger
poise again to suckle to sing to kiss—
one who'll be carrion
                    one who'll carry on

A SONG FOR WOMEN
(after Audre Lorde)

Because you belong to no one
because you dig trenches
because you figure in the dreams of people
who do not even know you
because you are beautiful—all of you—sing
because you have sons who might learn
to honor wind the way you praise
the sound of mouths at your breast
because you love the smell that rises
from your own blood between your legs
because you love women beautiful
women—all of you—sing
because you roil sand and tide and eyes
because cities throb with your bodies
because you burn drink fire belong
to no one—sing—beautiful women
all of you because you give
a thousand hours of short nights
to touch you—because you touch I only hope
to meet you slowly—one by one—
in the sweet blackberry rawness of your La La Las

THE BASQUE NOSE

I may as well be invisible
when Curtis says to Idoia his wife
That Basque nose
Let me touch that nose
and she lets him
and I'm surprised I don't
repeat him: Let *me* touch that nose
even though I've thought more often
of her chin—what I would abandon
to touch the line along
the muscle of her neck
to the small ridge below her ear—
a place which has no simple word
even in the half dozen languages
we choose not to speak in that room

Curtis—one of the most benign
men I know except for one
New Year's when he got drunk and vaulted
his six-foot-four Iowa-farmboy frame
over the dinner table to stomp
the gum out of some brute
pushing up on Idoia
But do you blame him?
The brute I mean
for blabbing anything
the liquor he mistook
for muse inspired him to say
just to hear Idoia speak—her vowels
thin cool and round as céntimos
dropped in a beggar's hand

I smoke on their front patio
Idoia stops in the kitchen
And I hold my cigarette
to the window between us—
how (for a moment) she purses
her mouth near the glass
a mock gesture too much
like a kiss for me to ignore

After dinner Curtis Idoia and I drink
wine which gives me courage
to practice my Spanish I think about
the difference between saber and conocer
conjugating each verb beginning
in first person New Jersey familiar
So when Curtis gets drunk
and kisses his wife's shoulders
they both close their eyes and I'm still
muttering *I know . . . You know . . . He knows . . .*

LITANY OF THE MISSING CHEEKBONE

When you kiss me
You speak rocks and sands
You speak salt sleet sampaguita
You speak wax and mosque and lung

You speak honeysuckle You speak fuck
You speak bite
                You speak stone
You speak the five syllables of my fingers
You speak me
                speaking you Love
you speak me
                into my mouth—
you belly/you tongue/you rain

IGNEOUS

Within the body too there's grit
sawdust slag The hard-at-work
capillaries the chugging veins And deeper:

the dark quarries where slabs of sun
gird the ragged digs of the body's rock
the handsome jags How can I arrive

at the innermost core
the sun-absent center of me:
slow flowing tectonic molten
and luminous?

BE REMINDED OF NOTHING

And since this is a poem that knows I can't take you
to Paris would you settle

for Hoboken and another gusty evening: a restaurant
with Havana in its name

—arroz amarrillo con pollo calamares crispy plantains
tempting me to eat in small bites

what's left so I could listen to you all night
explain why we savor

grease and fat-slick food listing in no particular order
everything delicious that would stop a man's heart

Would you sit for those two hours and not once
place your hand on mine Would you

laugh hard with me without knowing your grandfather
in eleven days will die Then

will you say nothing about him—just
dance with me drunk in a city that's threatened

to spin us on its twisted axis a dozen times on any
given night Will you and I each go home

having forgotten for a little while the sudden
lunge of engines thousands of miles away

guns the quick click of empty chambers so
if I came to you—

would you get up—in the middle of sleep—and open the door
Would you let me in

This used to be a poem that ended
in a taxi—a polite kiss on the cheek Forget that

Now this is a poem that claims love is relative
If I could travel near the speed of light

I would fly into the headwind's chill: an excuse for us
to slip into a bar where

you'd sip from a glass of cheap Chablis and theorize
about odd socks and bad mambo partners but

the only way I can speak to you is pretend I don't want
to kneel beside you and listen to you breathe in the dark

If once more you sat with me in a crowded corner over drinks
would you forget everything—but

the long line of your neck Would you tell me
what you want to hide

when a man like me comes along
Would you let me touch you

there

BETTER

What's ruined
you shouldn't see right away
It should take all the mornings
you've ever spent bawling
over something small
long before you even know true grief
It should take the first moment
you watch your mother place
her lips on the open mouth
of your father dropped
on your corridor floor
until she breathes him back to life
It should take that whole night
and the next eleven hundred to follow
when you've earned
the patience of thieves your own
teeth already begun to rot from
your gums the ache
in your ankles your knees your hip
It should take some terrible song
and the rum-sweet sway
of a woman's body you hold
against yours

Brothers
on nights like this we dance
because we don't know any better

Thank God we don't or else
we all might live forever
sitting down

For Steve, Glenn, and Tee

POEM

It takes a whole lotta sturdy faith hey.
  —June Jordan

Takes stones and a hole dug	deep Takes
a knot in the back and shoulders	slumped Takes
a whole lotta fallen	
trees dead wood dry	brush Takes
genuflection at Black	Rock Takes
a psalm in the valley	blown Takes
a little sleep and one bad	dream
to wake up crying open my eyes	
and sing:	Damn—
enough stars up there to pin up	
the whole black	sky Takes
one good	breeze Takes
a god with broad hands and a breast	
soft enough for me to lay my	head To lay
my head	takes
prayer:	
Thank you for dirt	
Thank you for stubborn oak roots	
Thank you for the trickle spring	
for the winged shadow circling	
without a name for sweat to cool me	*down* Takes
earth and	lake Takes
the night	Takes
the stiff light by	moons Takes
fire to warm my feet and a dragon	
I can't	see Takes
a whole lotta faith—sturdy sturdy faith	hey

PICK-UP LINE ENDING WITH A PRAYER

When I tell la Colombiana I first met
a week before *Tu nombre*
se queda conmigo I know
this is a bad idea but
she doesn't stop me
with her stock stone stare
that sends away every other man
who's tried to speak to her tonight
I pull up my left sleeve
to show the sea and sun
tattooed on my forearm then
point and say her name
Mar-i-sol She smiles
I don't tell her the tattoo is a myth
of creation: a bird's trick to yoke
heavens and ocean in a titanic
barroom brawl: the ancient scrap
which has begotten all the continents
of desire: even the four-foot liquor-stained
ellipsis where Marisol and I will stand
at the corner of a crowded New Jersey dance floor
some 500 millenia later

I need to know something
about the legacy of beauty she inherits
the way a coastline inherits salt
I have yet to learn the catalog of unloved
gestures a woman lets no one read
I have yet to understand grace
is not the absence of awkwardness

but an accumulation of so many
quirks the body finds a way
to make them happen all at once

Lord my job tonight is to fashion lies
as with any life-long ambition
I may not deserve to fall in love But
let this be true—the beginning
in which there was only an ocean and a star
and a little pain we called distance
Let there be a bird with nowhere to alight
who taunts the heavens to water
who riles waters to the heavens
Let there be mar-y-sol Let there be land
and one day let it contain a dance floor There
let me recognize human grace when I see it:
every mis-step and slip
every foible and fuck-up
Let me know them
like the first errors of the sea

Notes

"The Overnight Ferry"
This poem first appeared as part of a collaborative project with painter Kim Krause. He solicited one piece each from nine writers, including myself, for his series of nine oils on canvas, titled "Greek Variations." The show originally ran at the Linda Schwartz Gallery, Cincinnati.

"Poem"
The epigraph is from a letter sent to me by June Jordan in 1998.

"A Song for Women"
I borrow from Audre Lorde's "Sequelae": "I figure in the dreams of people/who do not even know me"

Patrick Rosal is the author of the chapbook *Uncommon Denominators,* winner of the Palanquin Poetry Series Award. His poems have been published in the journals *Footwork: The Paterson Literary Review, Columbia: A Journal of Literature and Art, The Literary Review* as well as the anthologies *Eros Pinoy, The Beacon Best 2001, Screaming Monkeys,* and *The NuyorAsian Anthology.* His collaborations include work with composer Robert Paterson, painter Kim Krause, and Allied Motion, dance company in residence at Penn State Altoona. A featured reader and performer at many venues in and out of New York City, from Boston to Daytona Beach, he teaches literature and creative writing at Bloomfield College.